CAMBRIDGE Global English Starters

Learner's Book C

Kathryn Harper & Gabrielle Pritchard

Welcome!

Cambridge Global English is a ten-stage course for learners of English as a Second Language (ESL). The ten stages range from the beginning of primary (Starters–Stage 6) to the end of lower secondary (Stages 7–9). It is ideal for all international ESL learners, and particularly for those following the Cambridge Primary and Lower Secondary English as a Second Language Curriculum Frameworks, as it has been written to adhere to these frameworks.

In addition to Learner's Book C, *Cambridge Global English Starters Activity Book C* provides supplementary support and practice. *Cambridge Global English Starters Fun with Letters and Sounds C* offers intensive practice in reading and writing of the upper- and lower-case letters learnt in lesson 4a of each unit. Comprehensive support for teachers is available in the *Cambridge Global English Starters Teacher's Resource*.

The following icons are used in this Learner's Book:

Audio track number reference

Differentiation

Personalisation

Critical thinking

For further explanation please refer to the teacher's resource.

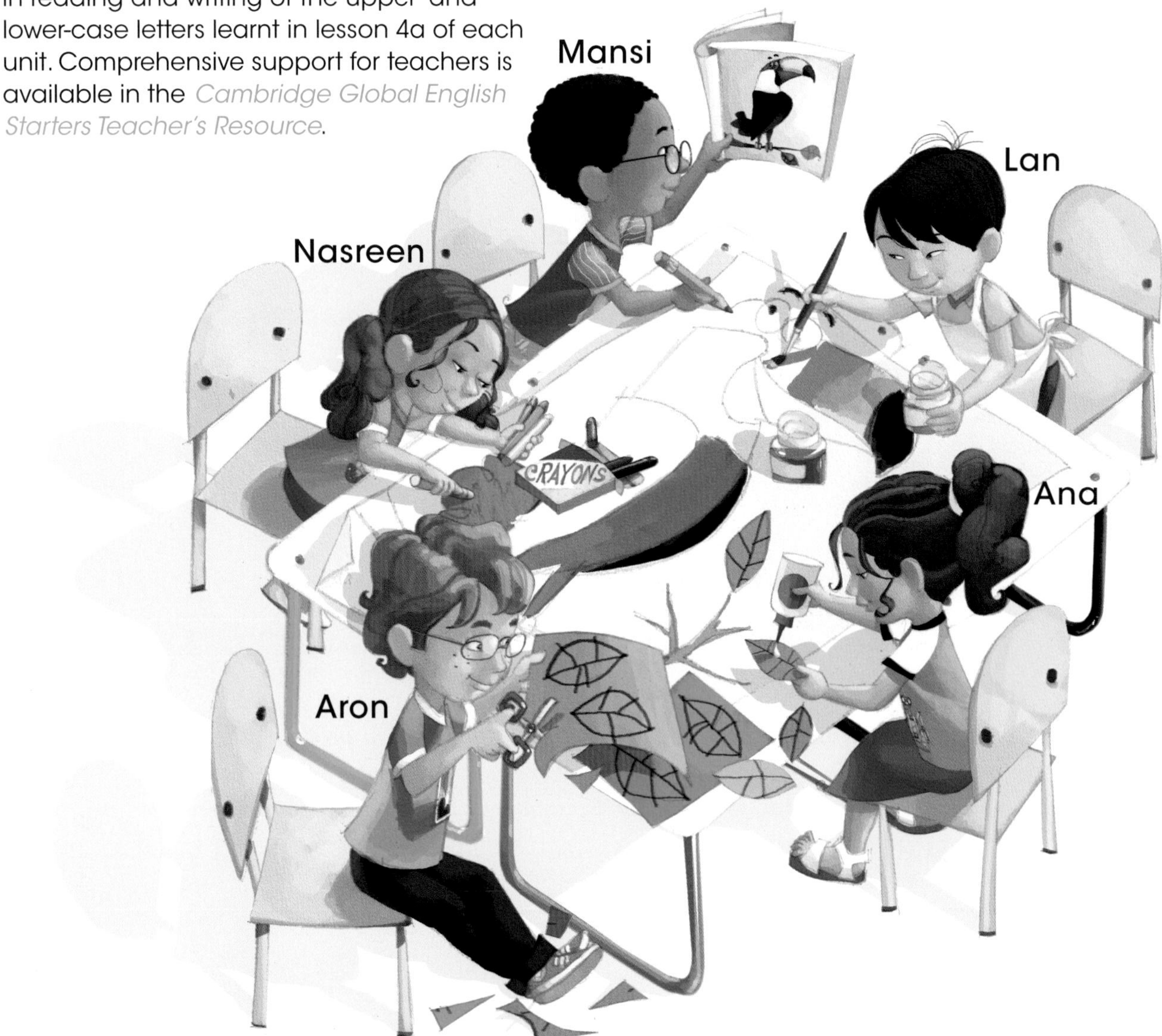

Contents

7 Homes!

8 What do clothes tell us?

9 In my garden

Please see the teacher's resource for complete scope and sequence.

7 Homes!

1 Think about it What's in your home?

1 Chant and clap.

Is it in the bedroom or bathroom?
Is it in the living room or kitchen?
Where's the teeny, tiny mouse
... hiding in our house?

2 What can you see? Explore.

Unit 7 Lesson 1 Words: bedroom, bathroom, living room, kitchen, flat, house **Language:** This is my (bedroom) **Speaking:** talk about the big picture, game
Listen and respond: chant, stick, say

3 Listen, find and say.

Listen again and stick.

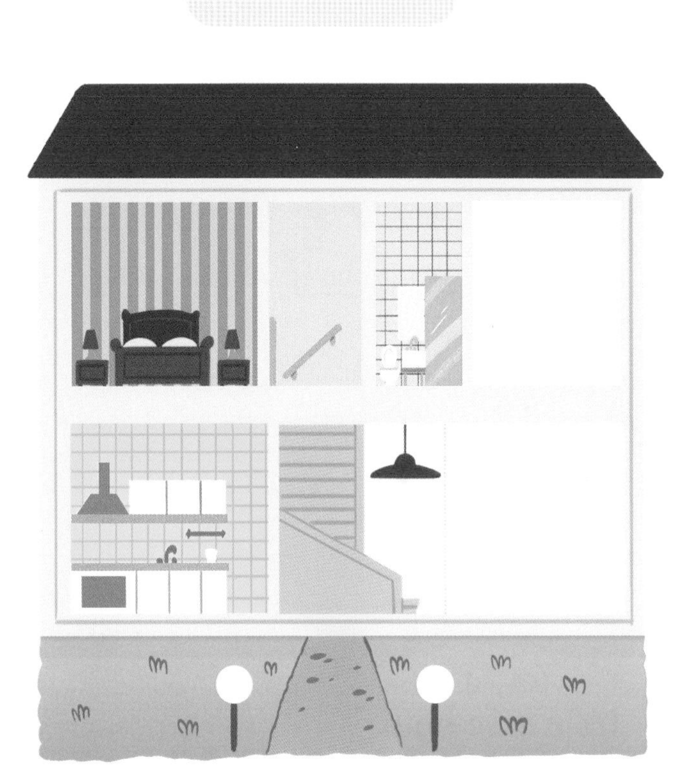

kitchen living room bathroom bedroom

4 Play the game.

Think of a room. Mime. Your friends guess the room.

Our wonderful home

3 1 **Listen and follow the story.**
Find the rooms in the story.

Unit 7 Lesson 2 words: tree, sofa, table, cooker, stairs, shower, bath, toy box, pet, inside, outside **Language:** There's a (cooker) in the (kitchen). There are (four) chairs) **Listen/Read:** story **Speaking:** acting out story, sharing

5
What's this room?
Look! There are 4 chairs and a table. Guess!

6
Oh, there's a cooker. It's the kitchen!

7
Look! Stairs. Let's go.

8
Wow! A bathroom. It's outside!
There's a bath **and** a shower.

Unit 7 Lesson 2 words: tree, sofa, table, cooker, stairs, shower, bath, toy box, pet, inside, outside **Language:** There's a (cooker) in the (kitchen). There are (four) chairs)
Listen/Read: story **Speaking:** acting out story, sharing

2a What kind of house do the family live in?

2b Which room is outside?

2c What unusual homes do you know about?

3 Look at the story. Play a game.

4 Who doesn't like the new home?

Why? Why does she change her mind?

3 Talk about it What's in your house?

1a What's coming out of the plane?

Look and say.

1b Listen and match.

4

2 Choose a room in your house.

Play.

Unit 7 Lesson 3 black, white, knock, lock, geese, kittens **Language:** Is there a (chair) in your (living room)? Yes, there are (4) (green) (chairs). **Listen/say:** game, song

3a Listen and match the animals to the rooms.

3b Listen, sing and act out.

Song: Welcome to my animal home

Chorus:

Welcome to my animal home
Where you are never, ever alone.
On the door, knock, knock, knock,
Turn the key, open the lock.

In the bedroom,
On the little red bed,
There's a funny brown rabbit
Bouncing on his head.
Boing, boing, boing.

In the kitchen,
Sitting on the chairs,
There are 2 big
Hungry black bears.
Grrrr.

In the bathroom,
Can you hear them laugh?
There are 3 white geese
Splashing in the bath.
Honk! Honk! Honk!

In the living room,
Sinking in the sofa deep,
There are 4 orange kittens
Oh, so fast asleep.
Shhhhhh.

4a Let's learn our ABC

1a Listen, point and say.

1b Listen, find and trace.

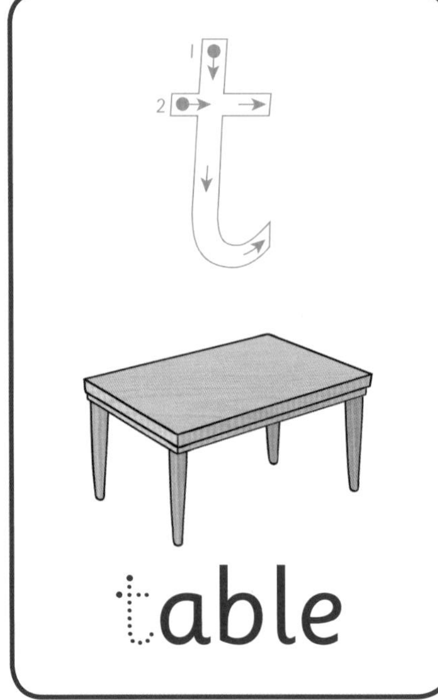

2a Say and write the missing letters.

square

_ired

_mell

_ree

_ad

_riangle

2b Listen and check.

2c Which letter is missing?

Say, join and check. Then write.

_mbrella

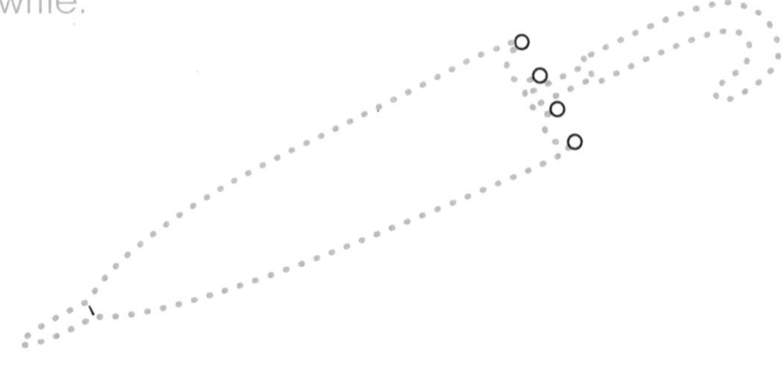

4b Let's learn our numbers

1 Look and say.

Write the numbers.

2a Listen and sing.

We can count up, up, up
We can count up to 10.
1, 2, 3, 4, 5,
6, 7, 8, 9, 10.

We can count down, down, down
We can count down again.
10, 9, 8, 7, 6,
5, 4, 3, 2, 1.

We can count up to 10,
And we can count down again.
H-o-o-r-a-y!

2b Count and write.

Seeing patterns

1a What is a pattern?

1b Look at these things.

How are they patterns?

1c Look at these patterns.

What kind are they? Tick ✓.

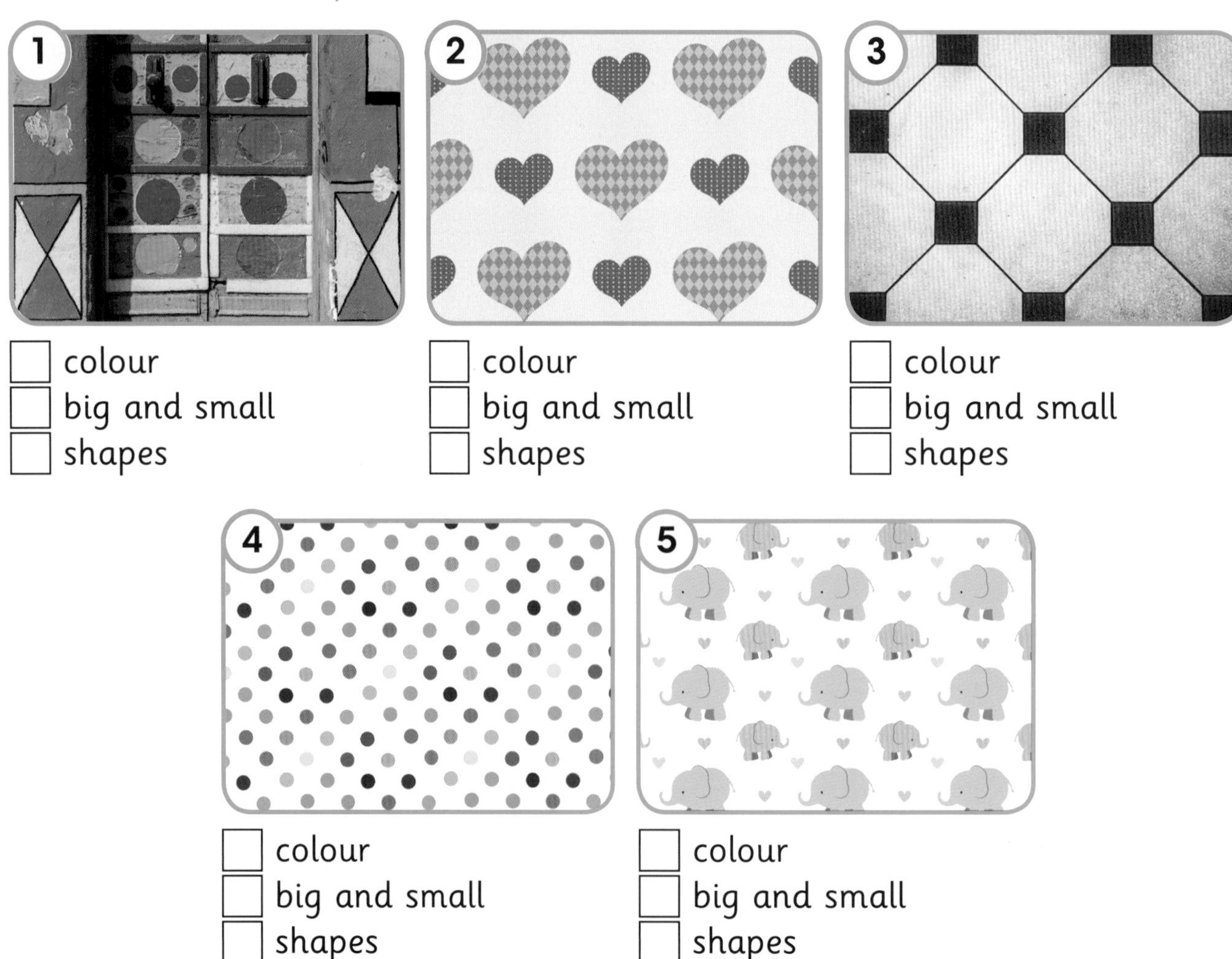

1d Find the patterns in the room.

1

2

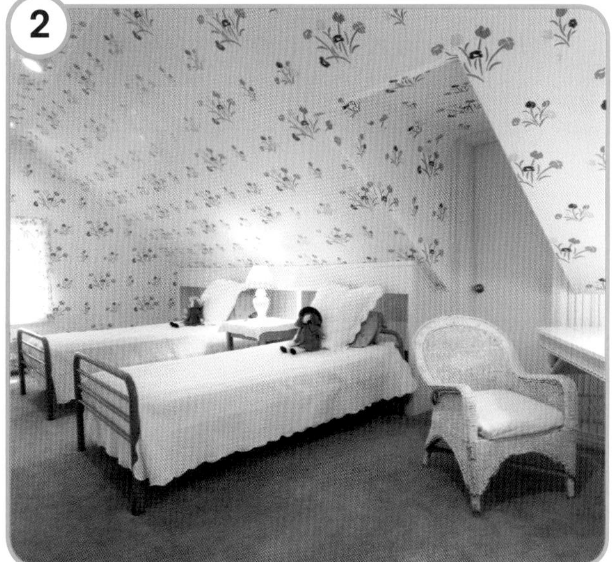

3

4

2a Explore your classroom.

Can you find patterns?
Draw or take pictures.

2b Show your patterns to the class.

Reflection

Which things create patterns in more than 1 way?

6 Our project

1 Design your own tree house.

Work with a friend.

Choose a picture. Plan the rooms.

2 Make your tree house picture.

Complete your picture. Write the names of the rooms.

3 Tell the class about your tree house.

Look what I can do!

I can:

- talk about homes
- follow and understand a story
- talk about what is in my house
- identify and say the letters and sounds **s**, **t**, **u**
- count to 10
- describe patterns

8 What do clothes tell us?

1 Think about it What clothes make you feel good?

11 **1 Chant and clap.**

A T-shirt, skirt and scarf,
A jumper, trousers and hat.
How do we pack all that?

2 What can you see?

Explore the picture.

Unit 8 Lesson 1 Words: t-shirt, jumper, trousers, skirt, scarf, hat **Language:** He's/She's wearing a (yellow T-shirt) **Speaking:** talk about the big picture, game **Listen and respond:** chant, stick, say

3 Listen and stick.

Then talk about the puppets.

4 Play the clothes game.

Make 2 teams. Race to find the right clothes.

What's Granny making?

13 **1 Listen and follow the story.**

Look at the first picture. What is Granny making?

5
A black hat!
Who is the hat for?
Who is the jumper for?
6
They're for the elephant!
It's winter and he doesn't
like the cold.
7
Now Elephant is
wearing the hat and
the jumper. He's nice
and warm.
8
That's a nice jumper.
I like that hat.

9
All the animals are asking for new clothes.
A pink skirt, please.
A blue scarf, please.
Purple trousers, please.
10
Now Granny is making trousers, a skirt and a scarf ...
11
... and I'm helping Granny.
12
Thank you very much!

2 Who is it?

Match and say.

3 Trace to match the clothes to the characters.

4 Why do the animals want. new clothes?

5 Listen and act out the story.

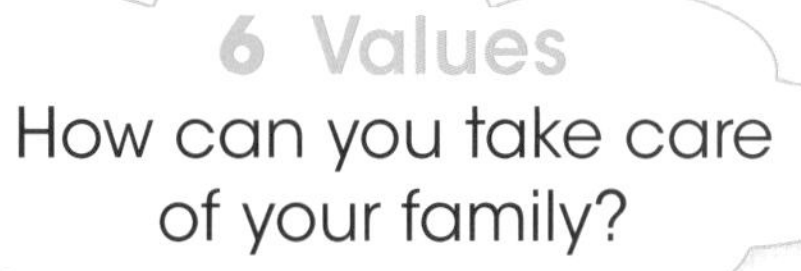

6 Values

How can you take care of your family?

3 Talk about it He's wearing a ...

1a What's missing? Say and stick.

1b Listen and say 'yes' or 'no'.

1c Say what the boy and girl are wearing.

1d What's the weather like for the girl and boy?

2a Look at the children's clothes and guess what the weather is like.

Circle and say.

2b What's the weather like today?

What are your friends wearing?

Unit 8 Lesson 3 Words: windy, rainy, sunny, sunglasses, jacket **Language:** He/she's wearing (a hat). What's the weather like? It's (sunny) today. **Listen/say:** game, song

Stickers for Unit 7 page 5

House

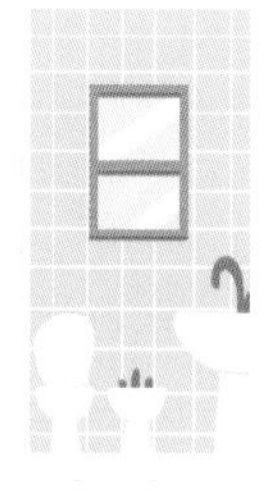

Stickers for Unit 8 page 19

Stickers for Unit 8 page 24

Stickers for Unit 9 page 33

Stickers for Unit 9 page 38

3 **Match to the verses.**
Then listen, sing and act out.

Song: Can I go out to play?

Please, please Mum,
Can I go out to play?
I don't know ...
It's cold today.
I'm wearing a hat.
Am I allowed to play?
Well. OK!

Please, please Mum,
Can I go out to play?
I don't know ...
It's windy today.
I'm wearing a jumper.
Am I allowed to play?
Well. OK!

Please, please Mum,
Can I go out to play?
I don't know ...
It's sunny today.
I'm wearing sunglasses.
Am I allowed to play?
Well. OK!

Please, please Mum,
Can I go out to play?
I don't know ...
It's rainy today.
I'm wearing a jacket.
Am I allowed to play?
Well. OK!

4a Let's learn our ABC

1a Listen, point and say.

1b Listen, find and trace.

2a Talk about the pictures.

Then listen, point and say.

2b Listen and write the missing letters.

4b Let's learn our numbers

1 How many?

Write the numbers.

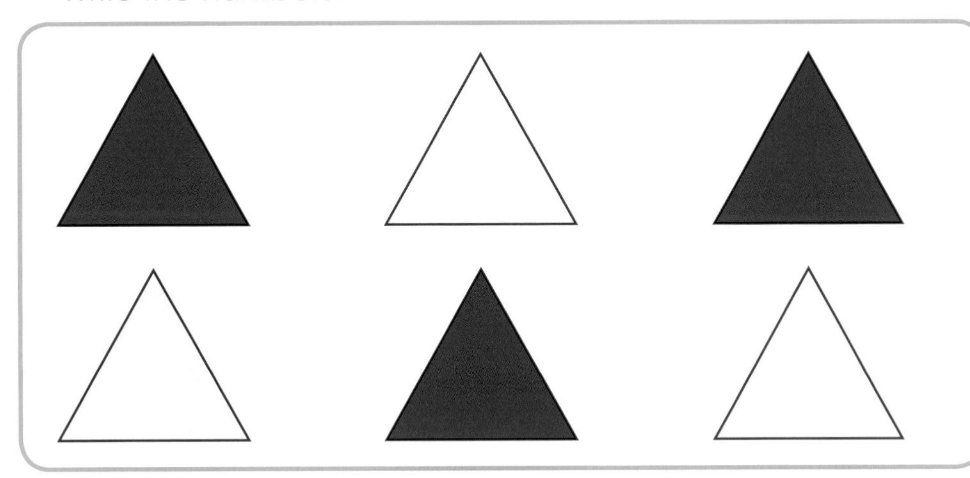

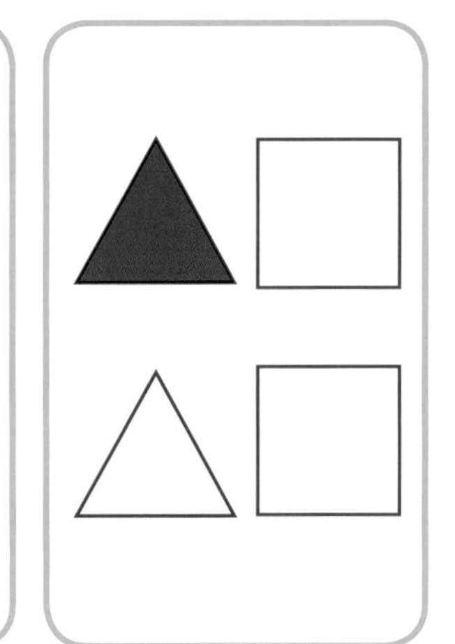

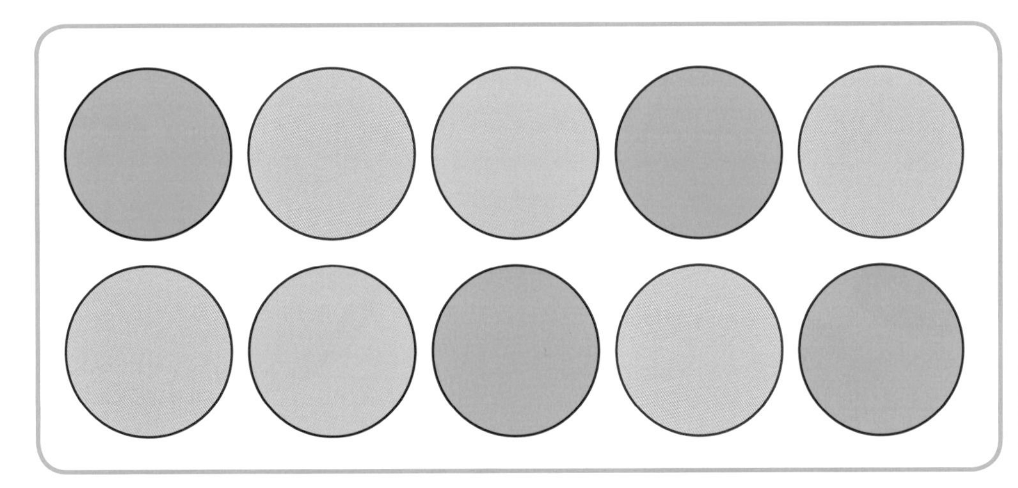

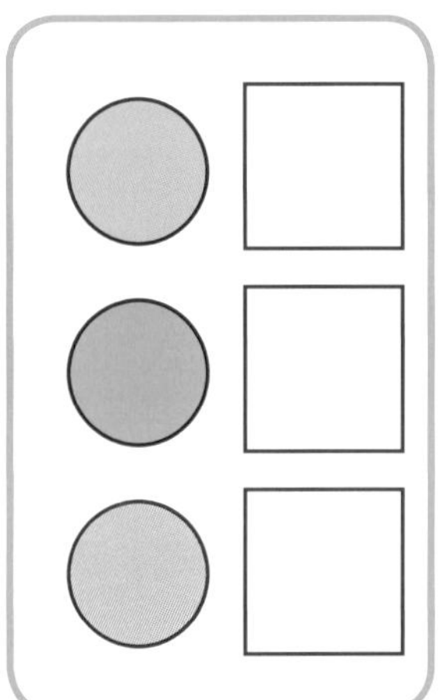

2 Add and write the answer.

1  ___ + ___ =

2  ___ + ___ =

3 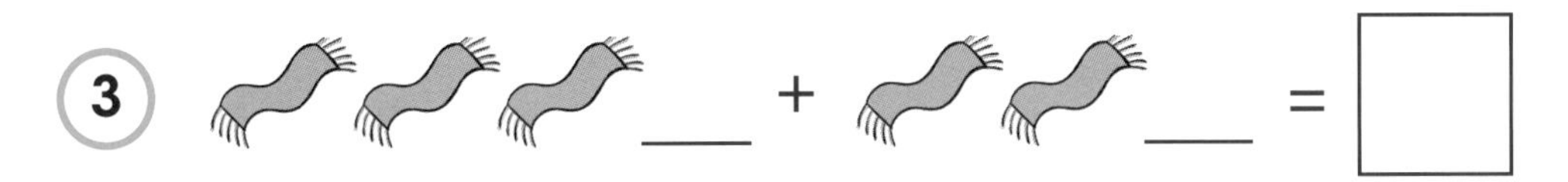 ___ + ___ =

4  ___ + ___ =

5 Find out more The clothes we wear each day

1a Think about your day.

When do you wear different clothes?

1b Listen and trace and follow the day.

What are the children wearing?

2a What are you wearing? Draw and colour.

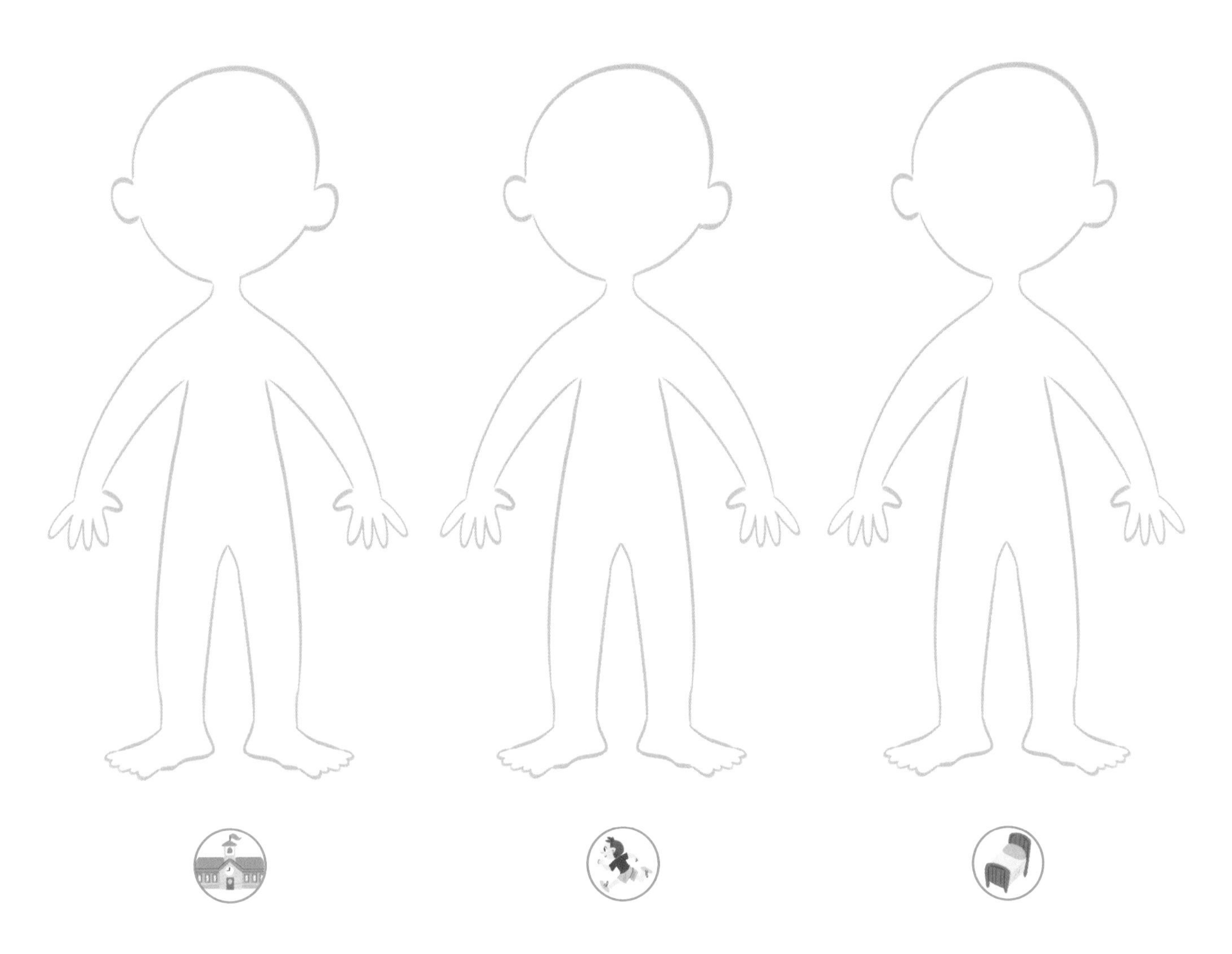

2b It's daytime and you're not at school.
What are you wearing?
Draw and tell the class.

Reflection

Why are some clothes good for playing in?

1 Design and make clothes.

2 Make a display.

3 Talk about your doll.

Look what I can do!

I can:

- talk about which clothes make us feel good
- talk about clothes
- follow and understand a story
- understand why we wear different clothes
- identify and say the letters and sounds **v**, **w**, **x**
- count to 10 and add numbers

9 In my garden

1 Think about it What can we find in the garden?

22 1 Chant and clap.

On a plant near the pond,
I see a spider, bird and bee,
And a little ladybird climbing a tree.

2 What can you see?

Explore the picture.

Unit 9 Lesson 1 **Words:** plant, pond, spider, bird, bee, ladybird, butterfly **Speaking:** talk about the big picture, game **Listen and respond:** chant, stick, say

3 Listen and stick.

Then talk about the picture.

4 Play the bug game.

Choose a leader. Tell your bugs what to do.

Jack and the beanstalk

24 **1a Listen and follow the story.**

Look at the pictures on this page. What does the beanstalk come from?

1b Can you find 4 little bugs in the story?

1 Jack and his mum are poor.

Mum.
Cow is hungry.
There is no food.
Take Cow to market.
Moo!

2 A man sees Jack.

The man gives Jack 6 beans.

3 Mum is angry.

She throws the beans in the garden.

4 The next day.

5

Jack climbs up.

6

Next to the beanstalk is a **giant** house. Jack goes inside.

7

He sees a gold bird on the table.

8

Jack hides under the table.

9

Give me a gold egg, bird!

10

Jack jumps out.

11

Jack climbs down.

12

2 Look, choose and trace.

Mum man

Giant Jack

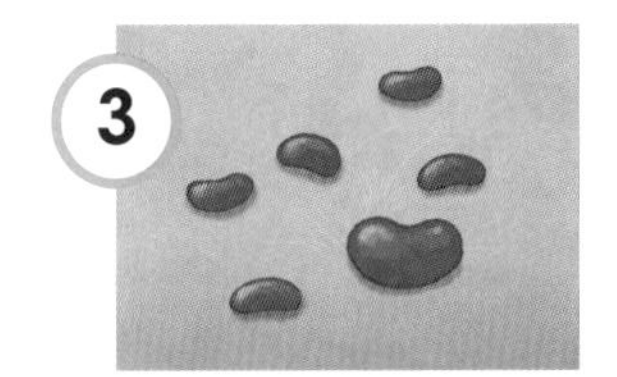

beanstalk beans

bird egg

up down

3a Why does Mum like the egg?

3b What will Mum and Jack do with the egg?

4 Make a big beanstalk.

5 Listen and act out the story.

6 Values

How can we be safe?

3 Talk about it Where are they?

1a Listen, point and say.

1b Where's the bee? Read and match.

in next to on under

2 Where are they?

Listen and stick. Then say.

3a Look and match.

Then listen and sing.

Song: In my garden

In my garden, I can see
A purple butterfly
Under the tree.
I'm looking round my garden,
Looking round my garden.

In my garden, I can hear
A buzzing bee
Next to my ear ...
I'm looking round my garden,
Looking round my garden.

In my garden, I can see
A yellow bird
In the tree ...
I'm looking round my garden,
Looking round my garden.

In my garden, I can see
A big, black spider
On my knee.
EEEE!
I'm running out of my garden,
Running out of my garden!

3b Listen and draw.

Then listen, sing and act out.

4a Let's learn our ABC

1a Listen, point and say.

1b Listen, find and trace.

2a Look and guess.
Then join the dots.

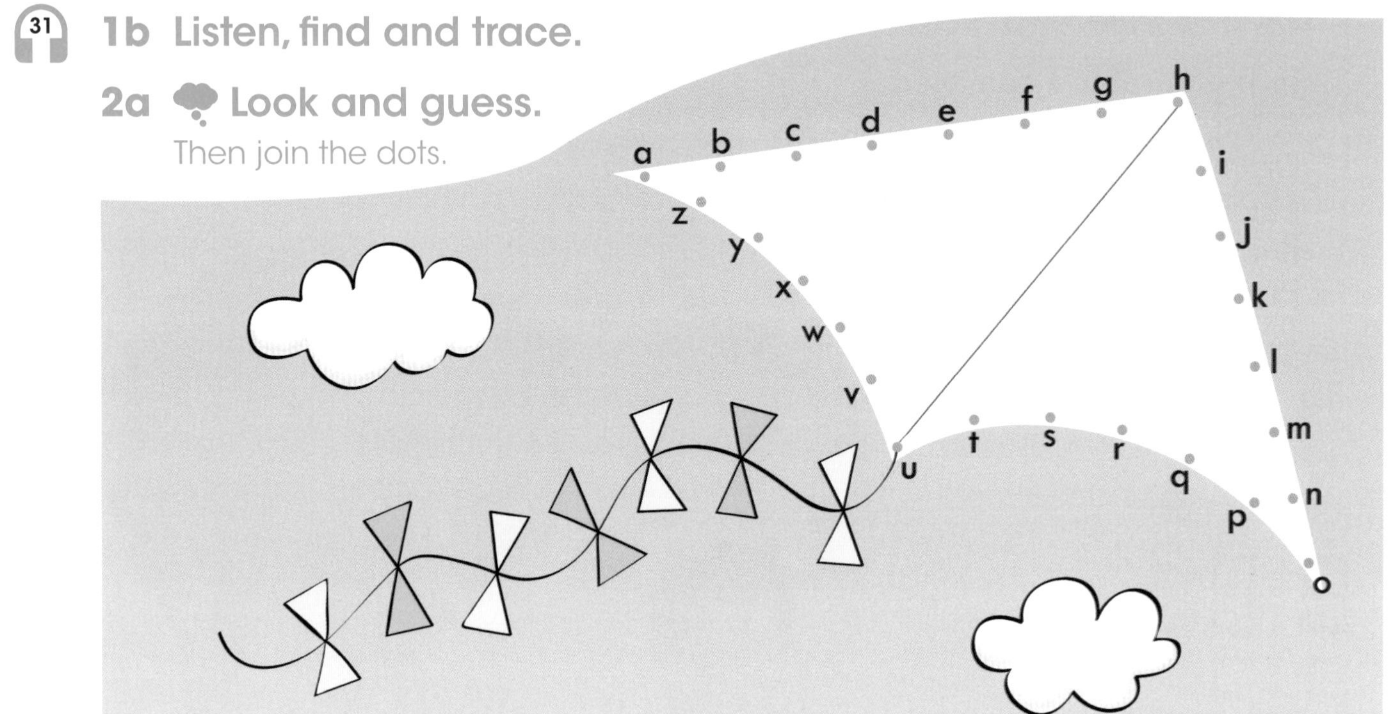

2b Complete the sentence, then colour.

It's a _ellow _ _ _ _.

3 Listen and do the alphabet rap.

Unit 9 Lesson 4 **Letters/sounds:** y, z **Words:** yellow, zoo **Numbers:** 1–10, adding on 1, 2 and 3 **Listen/say:** alphabet words, alphabet rap, number song

4b Let's learn our numbers

1 How many animals?

Write the numbers.

2 How many?

Write the numbers.

5 Find out more What comes from eggs? 

1a What comes from eggs?

Match.

egg

no egg

1b Talk about the animals.

Birds come from eggs.

2a Find the eggs in the picture.

2b Match the animals to the eggs.

2c Say where the eggs are found.

Reflection

What is similar about animals that come from eggs?

6 Our project

1 Go on a minibeast hunt.

Do a minibeast survey outside.

2 Make a class graph.

Put the minibeasts on the graph.

3 Talk about your results.

Look what I can do!

I can:

- talk about what we can find in the garden
- follow and understand a story
- talk about where things are
- identify and say the letters and sounds **y**, **z**
- say and write the alphabet
- add 1, 2 or 3
- talk about what comes from eggs
- talk about minibeasts/small animals

What can we remember?

1 Listen and draw lines.

  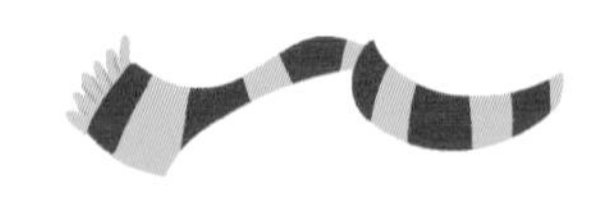 

  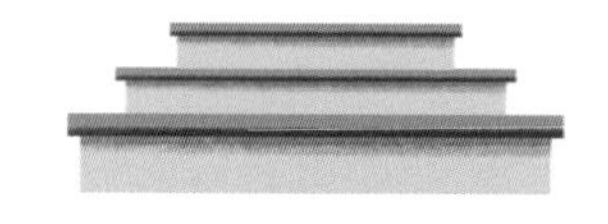 

2 Listen and say.

Then trace or tick ✓ the correct answer.

1	☐ bedroom	☐ bathroom	☐ living room
2	☐ bathroom	☐ living room	☐ garden
3	☐ kitchen	☐ bedroom	☐ living room
4	☐ bathroom	☐ bedroom	☐ kitchen
5	☐ garden	☐ kitchen	☐ living room
6	☐ bedroom	☐ living room	☐ bathroom

3 Listen and tick ✓ the box.

1

a ☐ b ☐ c ☐

2

a ☐ b ☐ c ☐

3

a ☐ b ☐ c ☐

4

a ☐ b ☐ c ☐

5

a ☐ b ☐ c ☐